COSTA BRAVA TRAVE

Your Ultimate Travel Companion: Exploring Costa Brava's Beaches and Seaside Towns

Diana C. Hopkins

All rights reserved. No part of this publication may be reproduced, distributed, or transmitted in any form or by any means, including photocopying, recording, or other electronic or mechanical methods, without the prior written permission of the publisher, except in the case of brief quotations embodied in critical reviews and certain other noncommercial uses permitted by copyright law.

Copyright © Diana C. Hopkins, 2024.

TABLE OF CONTENT

CHAPTER 1: INTRODUCTION TO COSTA BRAVA — 4

- Overview of Costa Brava — 7
- Why Visit Costa Brava — 11
- Geography and Climate — 14
- History and Culture — 17
- Local Customs and Etiquette — 21

CHAPTER 2: PLANNING YOUR COSTA BRAVA ADVENTURE — 25

- Best time to visit Costa Brava — 29
- Visa and Travel Documents — 32
- Currency and Essential Information — 34
- Getting Around Costa Brava: Airports, Trains, Buses, Car Rentals, and Local Transportation Options — 37

CHAPTER 3: ACCOMMODATION OPTIONS — 41

- 5 Budget Hotels and Guesthouses — 44
- 5 Luxury Resorts — 45

CHAPTER 4: TOP ATTRACTIONS IN COSTA BRAVA — 48

Beaches and Coastal Towns	53
Natural Parks	58

CHAPTER 5: EXPLORING COSTA BRAVA'S REGIONS — 61

Costa Brava's Coastal Gems	64

CHAPTER 6: CULINARY DELIGHTS — 68

Wine & Dine in Style	71
Recommended Restaurants	75
Festivals & Celebrations	78

CHAPTER 7: ACTIVITIES AND ADVENTURES — 84

Water Sports and Beach Activities	88
Hiking and Cycling Routes	92

CHAPTER 8: NIGHTLIFE — 97

Shopping	100

CHAPTER 9: PRACTICAL INFORMATION — 104

CHAPTER 10: BEYOND COSTA BRAVA — 109

Insider Tips And Local Insights	112
Useful Phrases	116

CHAPTER 1: INTRODUCTION TO COSTA BRAVA

Imagine a coastline where rugged cliffs plunge into turquoise waters, where charming fishing villages whisper tales of a bygone era, and where vibrant towns pulsate with a joie de vivre that lingers long after your visit. This, dear traveler, is the magic of Costa Brava, a captivating region on Spain's northeastern coast waiting to unveil its treasures to you. Within the pages of this 2024 Costa Brava Travel Guide, we invite you to embark on a journey that transcends the ordinary. Picture yourself strolling along cobbled streets adorned with colorful flowers, the scent of fresh seafood wafting from bustling markets.

Imagine the thrill of exploring hidden coves accessible only by boat, the crystalline waters beckoning you for a refreshing dip. This guide is your key to unlocking the secrets of Costa Brava.

We'll be your companion as you wander through medieval towns steeped in history, their ancient walls whispering stories of kings and knights. We'll guide you to secluded beaches, where the sound of waves crashing against the shore is the only symphony you need. Venture with us into the lush hinterland, where volcanic landscapes offer breathtaking vistas and charming villages beckon with authentic experiences. Whether you crave the thrill of water sports, the serenity of hidden coves, or the indulgence of world-class cuisine, Costa Brava caters to every desire.

This 2024 edition ensures you have the most up-to-date information on festivals, events, and hidden gems, allowing you to craft an itinerary that perfectly blends cultural immersion with relaxation and adventure.

So, pack your bags, open your heart to new experiences, and let us whisk you away to the captivating embrace of Costa Brava. Within these pages lies the promise of an unforgettable journey – a tapestry woven with sun, sea, and the vibrant soul of this extraordinary region.

Overview of Costa Brava

1. Scenic Coastline: Costa Brava runs along the Mediterranean Sea for almost 160 kilometers, with stunning cliffs, secret coves, and pure

sandy beaches. The rocky beauty of the coastline is defined by crystal-clear seas and spectacular views.

2. **Charming Coastal Towns:** Discover the little fishing villages and beach towns that dot the Costa Brava coastline. From the colorful mansions of Cadaqués to the historic lanes of Tossa de Mar, each town has its own distinct charm and personality.

3. **Cultural Heritage:** Costa Brava is rich in history, with ancient ruins, medieval castles, and Romanesque cathedrals dotted across the area. Explore the medieval stronghold of Pals, the ancient Greek and Roman remains of Empúries, and the Salvador Dalí House Museum in Portlligat.

4. **Outdoor Activities:** Nature lovers and outdoor enthusiasts will have much to do in Costa Brava. Explore the mountainous coastline on hiking paths like the Camí de Ronda, snorkel or scuba dive in crystal-clear seas, or participate in water sports like kayaking, windsurfing, and sailing.

5. **Gastronomic joys:** Enjoy the gastronomic joys of Costa Brava, which is recognized for its fresh seafood, Catalan cuisine, and world-class restaurants. Visit beach restaurants and tapas bars to try local delicacies including paella, fideuà (similar to paella but prepared with noodles), and suquet de peix (fish stew).

6. **Art and Culture:** Learn about the creative tradition of Costa Brava, which has inspired generations of artists, authors, and filmmakers.

Explore the Dalí Theatre-Museum in Figueres, the historic alleyways of Girona, and the region's bustling cultural culture.

7. Festivals and Events: Throughout the year, Costa Brava hosts a variety of festivals and events that provide a vibrant environment. From traditional events like the Festa Major in each town to music festivals, cuisine fairs, and cultural exhibits, Costa Brava has something going on at all times.

Why Visit Costa Brava

1. **Stunning Natural Beauty:** Costa Brava has some of Europe's most magnificent coastal vistas, including steep cliffs, secret coves, and pristine beaches that line the Mediterranean Sea. Whether you're looking for sun-kissed beaches or gorgeous hiking paths, Costa Brava has plenty of natural beauty to discover.

2. **Rich Cultural Heritage:** Costa Brava has a rich cultural heritage, ranging from ancient ruins and medieval castles to attractive villages and historic towns. Discover the region's creative past at museums and galleries, walk through gorgeous towns with cobblestone streets, and participate in local customs and festivals.

3. **Adventure Adventures:** Costa Brava's diversified landscape and pleasant temperature make it an ideal destination for adventure enthusiasts. Whether you prefer hiking, cycling, water sports, or just relaxing on the beach, Costa Brava offers limitless chances for adventure and discovery.

4. **Gastronomic joys:** Savor the gastronomic joys of Costa Brava, which is famous for its fresh

seafood, Catalan cuisine, and world-class restaurants. Costa Brava's gastronomic trip ranges from traditional tapas bars to Michelin-starred dining experiences, delighting both foodies and gourmet aficionados.

5. Cultural Events and Festivals: Throughout the year, Costa Brava offers a number of cultural events, festivals, and celebrations that highlight the region's rich legacy and lively culture. From music festivals and gourmet fairs to traditional fiestas and religious processions, Costa Brava hosts a variety of events to amuse and inspire tourists.

6. Sustainable tourism Initiatives: In recent years, Costa Brava has made substantial efforts to promote sustainable tourism practices and environmental protection. By 2024, you can

support local projects aimed at preserving the region's natural beauty and cultural history for future generations to enjoy.

Geography and Climate

1. Geography: Costa Brava is situated in northeastern Catalonia, Spain, and stretches along the Mediterranean coastline from the French border to Blanes. The landscape is

defined by craggy cliffs, rocky headlands, secret coves, and sandy beaches. Inland, the terrain includes undulating hills, verdant woods, and lovely towns tucked amid olive trees and vineyards.

2. Coastline: The Costa Brava coastline is famous for its dramatic beauty, with sheer cliffs plummeting into the blue seas of the Mediterranean Sea. Along the coast, tourists will discover a variety of sandy beaches, pebbly coves, and rocky coasts, each with its own distinct appeal and landscape. Notable coastal features include the Cap de Creus peninsula, the Medes Islands archipelago, and the Bay of Roses.

3. Climate: Costa Brava has a Mediterranean climate, with hot, dry summers and moderate,

rainy winters. Summers are long and bright, with temperatures ranging between 25°C and 30°C (77°F to 86°F). The Mediterranean Sea's warm waters make it a great location for swimming and water sports throughout the summer. Winters are warm, with temperatures ranging from 10°C to 15°C (50°F to 59°F), however rain is more typical throughout this season.

4. Microclimates: Because of its diverse geography and closeness to the Pyrenees mountains, Costa Brava has microclimates that vary greatly from one location to the next. Coastal locations often have a more moderate environment, but inland regions may suffer lower temperatures and more rainfall. The region's diversified terrain, which includes

various nature reserves and protected areas, adds to its high biodiversity.

History and Culture

1. Ancient History: Human settlements on the Costa Brava may be traced back to prehistoric times. The Iberians, Greeks, and Romans

occupied the region and left archeological remains as ruins, fortifications, and amphitheaters.

2. Medieval Period: In the Middle Ages, Costa Brava was part of the Kingdom of Catalonia, which eventually became the Crown of Aragon. The area saw the development of medieval castles, cathedrals, and walled towns, many of which still exist today. The medieval town of Girona, with its well-preserved Jewish Quarter and Romanesque Cathedral, is a testimony to this era.

3. Renaissance and Baroque Eras: During the Renaissance and Baroque eras, Costa Brava saw a surge in arts and culture, with the development of palaces, houses, and churches embellished with beautiful decorations and

architectural elements. The architecture of places like Palafrugell and Palamós reflects this era's heritage.

4. **Modern History:** During the twentieth century, Costa Brava saw substantial changes as tourism and coastal development increased. Fishing villages were turned into resort towns, and tourism became a significant economic engine in the area. Today, Costa Brava is well-known for its bustling cultural scene, gastronomic pleasures, and outdoor activities.

5. **Cultural legacy:** Costa Brava's cultural legacy is evident in its customs, festivals, and culinary traditions. Visitors may attend local festivities such as the Festa Major, which honors each town's patron saint with parades, music, and fireworks. The gastronomic landscape in the

area focuses on Catalan cuisine, including fresh seafood, olive oil, and wines from local wineries.

6. Artistic Legacy: The Costa Brava region's natural beauty and scenic vistas have inspired generations of painters, authors, and filmmakers. Salvador Dalí, the famed surrealist painter, lived and worked in the area, leaving behind an artistic legacy that may be studied in the Dalí Theatre-Museum in Figueres, among other venues.

Local Customs and Etiquette

1. Greetings: When meeting someone for the first time or entering a store or restaurant, it's normal to greet them with a handshake and a warm "Hola" (hello) or "Buenos días" (good morning), depending on the time. In more formal situations, a little nod or bow may be suitable.

2. **Personal Space:** Spaniards have a stronger feeling of personal space than other cultures. People often stand closer together during chats and keep eye contact to show that they are engaged.

3. **Meal Times:** Spaniards usually eat lunch between 1:00 and 3:00 PM, and supper between 8:00 and 10:00 PM. Restaurants may not be open for supper until later in the evening, so schedule your meals appropriately. It is also customary to linger over meals and have leisurely eating experiences with friends and family.

4. **Dining Etiquette:** When eating out, wait for the host or server to seat you. Keep in mind that tipping is less prevalent in Spain than in other countries, although a little tip (about 5-10%) for

excellent service is often appreciated. When you've completed your meal, it's polite to set your utensils parallel across the dish to show that you're done.

5. Respect for Siesta: In many regions of Spain, including Costa Brava, the siesta custom is still practiced, especially in smaller towns and rural areas. Businesses may shut during siesta hours (typically between 2:00 PM and 5:00 PM), and residents may take a break to relax or spend time with their families. Respect local norms by reducing noise levels during siesta hours and avoiding needless disturbances.

6. Dress Code: Costa Brava has a relaxed and informal vibe, yet it's vital to dress correctly while visiting religious sites or fancy restaurants. Shoulders and knees should be

covered in churches and cathedrals to show respect for religious traditions.

7. Language: Although many people in Costa Brava speak Catalan, Spanish is commonly known and spoken. Learning a few simple Spanish words, like "por favor" (please) and "gracias" (thank you), may go a long way toward demonstrating respect for the local culture.

CHAPTER 2: PLANNING YOUR COSTA BRAVA ADVENTURE

1. Choose Your Travel Dates: Determine when you want to visit Costa Brava depending on weather, local events, and your own schedule. Keep in mind that the main tourist season is normally between June and August, when the weather is nicest and most attractions are open, although costs may be higher and crowds bigger.

2. **Research Destinations and Attractions:** Explore Costa Brava's towns, beaches, and attractions. Consider your hobbies and preferences, whether you like historic sights, outdoor activities, gourmet experiences, or just resting on the beach. Girona, Tossa de Mar, Cadaqués, and Cap de Creus Natural Park are all must-see places.

3. **Create a schedule:** Based on your study, make a rough schedule of the sites you want to see and the activities you want to do each day. Make sure to account for travel time between sites and allow for flexibility in case you find additional sites or activities along the route.

4. **Reserve Accommodation:** Choose accommodations that fit your budget, tastes, and vacation style. Costa Brava has a variety of lodging alternatives, including hotels, resorts, vacation rentals, and campgrounds. Consider staying in several towns or places to get a sense of the region's variety.

5. **Arrange Transportation:** Plan how you'll go to Costa Brava and how you'll get about while there. If flying, look into flights to neighboring airports like Girona-Costa Brava Airport (GRO) or Barcelona-El Prat Airport (BCN). Renting a vehicle is a handy way to explore the area on your own, but there are also public transit choices like trains and buses.

6. **Pack Accordingly:** Pack clothes and necessities depending on the activities you want

to do and the time of year you'll be visiting. In addition

Best time to visit Costa Brava

1. **Summer (June to August):**

   - Peak tourist season with warm temperatures and sunny days.

   - Ideal for beachgoers and water sports enthusiasts.

   - Crowded beaches and higher accommodation prices.

- Many cultural events and festivals take place during this time.

2. Spring (April to May):

- Mild temperatures with blooming flowers and green landscapes.
- Less crowded than summer, making it a great time for sightseeing and outdoor activities.
- Ideal for hiking, cycling, and exploring Costa Brava's natural parks.
- Accommodation prices are generally lower compared to summer.

3. Autumn (September to November):

- Pleasant temperatures and fewer crowds than summer.
- Ideal for outdoor activities such as hiking and exploring historic towns.

- Harvest season for grapes and olives, offering opportunities to visit wineries and taste local products.

- Accommodation prices begin to decrease after the peak summer season.

4. Winter (December to February):

- Mild to cool temperatures with occasional rain.

- Quieter and less crowded than other seasons.

- Ideal for exploring Costa Brava's cultural attractions, museums, and art galleries.

- Some beach resorts and tourist facilities may close during the off-season.

- Winter holidays, including Christmas and New Year's Eve, bring festive celebrations and events.

Visa and Travel Documents

1. Schengen Visa: If you are a citizen of a country other than the European Union (EU), European Economic Area (EEA), or Switzerland, you may need a Schengen visa to visit Spain, including Costa Brava. The Schengen visa permits you to remain in the Schengen Area, including Spain, for up to 90 days within a 180-day period for tourist, business, or family trips.

2. Exemptions: Some nations waive visa requirements for short visits in the Schengen Area. Citizens of some countries, including the United States, Canada, Australia, and Japan, do not need a visa for visits of up to 90 days within a 180-day period for tourism or business. However, they must verify that their passport is

valid for at least three months after their planned stay.

3. **Passport Requirements:** To enter Spain, all passengers, regardless of country, must provide a valid passport. Your passport should be valid for at least three months after your planned stay. Make sure your passport has enough blank pages for entrance stamps.

4. **Other papers:** Depending on your nationality and the purpose of your trip, you may be required to present other papers such as evidence of adequate finances, travel insurance, hotel reservations, and a return ticket.

5. **Visa Application Process:** If you want a Schengen visa, you must apply for one at the Spanish embassy or consulate in your home

country or place of residency. The application procedure normally consists of filling out a visa application form, supplying needed papers, attending an interview (if applicable), and paying a visa fee.

6. Travel Insurance: It is suggested that you get travel insurance that covers medical expenditures, emergency medical evacuation, and trip cancellation/interruption for the length of your vacation to Costa Brava.

Currency and Essential Information

1. Currency: The Euro (EUR) is the official currency in Spain, including Costa Brava. Make sure you convert your money into Euros prior to your travel or withdraw cash from ATMs upon

arrival. Credit cards are generally accepted at most venues, but it's always a good idea to have some cash on hand for little purchases and in case you come into a place that doesn't take cards.

2. Language: The official languages of Costa Brava are Catalan and Spanish. While Catalan is the predominant language spoken in the region, most inhabitants also speak Spanish, particularly in tourist destinations. Although English is frequently spoken in tourist areas and hotels, learning a few basic Spanish phrases can help you converse with the locals.

3. Time Zone: Costa Brava is in the Central European Time Zone (CET), or UTC+1. Daylight Saving Time is observed from late March to late October, with clocks adjusted one hour forward.

4. Electricity: In Spain, the standard voltage is 230 volts at a frequency of 50 Hz. The power plugs and sockets used are Type F, however they also take Type C and E plugs. If your gadgets have various plug types, you may need a travel adaptor.

5. Safety: Costa Brava is typically a safe place for visitors, however it is important to follow normal safety measures. Keep your valuables safe, be alert of your surroundings, and avoid poorly lit or lonely locations, particularly at night.

6. Healthcare: Spain boasts a top-tier healthcare system, and emergency medical services are easily accessible. European Union citizens may access emergency medical care using a European Health Insurance Card (EHIC) or its

equivalent, the European Health Insurance Card (EH).

Getting Around Costa Brava: Airports, Trains, Buses, Car Rentals, and Local Transportation Options

1. Flying into Costa Brava

-Main Airport: Girona-Costa Brava Airport (GRO): This is the closest airport to the heart of Costa Brava, with connections to major European cities.

-Estimated Cost: Round Trip flights can range from €50 to €500+ depending on the origin city, season, and airline.

2. Train Travel

-RENFE: The Spanish national railway network, RENFE, operates frequent and reliable train services connecting Barcelona with major towns along the Costa Brava coast, including Blanes, Lloret de Mar, and Figueres.

-Estimated Cost: Tickets start around €10 for shorter journeys and increase for longer distances. Purchase tickets online or at train stations.

3. Bus Travel

-Regular Buses: Several bus companies operate routes connecting towns and villages along the Costa Brava coast.

-Barcelona to Costa Brava: Eurolines and Sagalés offer direct bus connections from Barcelona to major Costa Brava destinations.

Estimated Cost: Bus travel is generally a budget-friendly option, with tickets starting around €5 for shorter journeys.

4. Car Rentals
Renting a car offers the most flexibility for exploring Costa Brava at your own pace. Numerous car rental companies operate at Girona Airport and major towns.

-Estimated Cost: Daily car rentals start around €40 but can vary depending on car size, season, and demand. Consider factoring in gas prices when budgeting for car rentals.

5. Local Transportation
-Local Buses: Many towns have local bus networks connecting different areas within the town. Tickets are usually inexpensive and can

be purchased on board. (Estimated Cost: €1-€3 per ride)

-Taxis: Taxis are readily available in most towns and tourist areas. Fares are metered, and surcharges may apply for nighttime rides or luggage.

CHAPTER 3: ACCOMMODATION OPTIONS

1. **Luxury Resorts:** Hotel Camiral at PGA Catalunya Resort: From €200 per night - Hotel Santa Marta Resort: From €250 per night.

- Alàbriga Hotel & Home Suites: Starting at €300 per night.

2. Mid-Range Hotels: Hotel Trias (Palamós): Starting at €80/night.

   - Hotel Llevant (Llafranc): Starting at €100 per night.

   - Hotel Aigua Blava (Begur): Starting at €120 per night.

3. Budget Hotels and Guest Houses:

   - Hostal Alba (Calella de Palafrugell): Starting at €50 per night.

   - Hostal Blau (Blanes): Starting at €60 per night.

   - Hostal Sa Rascassa (Begur): Starting at €70 per night.

4. Holiday Apartments and Villas: Rent an apartment in seaside communities like Lloret de Mar, Tossa de Mar, and Cadaqués. Prices vary

by location, size, and amenities, but normally range between €60 and €150 each night.

- Rent villas with private pools and sea views in locations like Begur and Roses. Prices vary greatly depending on the size, location, and luxury amenities of the villa, but expect to spend between €150 and €500+ each night.

5. Hostels and backpacker accommodations:

- Hostel Calella (Calella de Palafrugell): Starting at €30 per night.

- Hostel Sant Jordi (Lloret de Mar): Starting at €20 per night.

- Bed and Go Apartments (Lloret de Mar): Starting at €25 per night.

5 Budget Hotels and Guesthouses

1. Hostal Alba (Calella de Palafrugell): Conveniently located near the beach and town center - Rooms are clean and comfortable with minimal facilities.

   - Prices start at €50 per night.

2. Hostal Blau (Blanes): Located in the middle of Blanes, close to the beach and attractions.

   - Affordable rooms with private bathrooms.

   Prices start at €60 per night.

3. Hostal Sa Rascassa (Begur): A charming guesthouse set in the countryside near Begur. - Rustic rooms with a quiet atmosphere. - Prices start at €70 per night.

4. Hostel Calella (Calella de Palafrugell): Affordable near the beach - Dormitory and

private rooms available - Prices start at €30 per night

5. **Hostel Sant Jordi (Lloret de Mar):** Conveniently located among nightlife and attractions in the bustling town.
   - Simple rooms with shared amenities.
   - Prices start at €20 per night.

5 Luxury Resorts

1. **Hotel Camiral at PGA Catalunya Resort:** Located in Caldes de Malavella near Girona - Offers a championship golf course, spa, and gourmet dining choices.

- Prices start at €200 per night.

2. **Hotel Santa Marta Resort:** Located in Lloret de Mar, overlooking the Mediterranean Sea - Provides exquisite rooms, a beach club, and a spa center - Prices begin at €250 per night.

3. **Alàbriga Hotel & Home rooms:** Located in S'Agaró, overlooking the magnificent Sant Pol Bay - Features luxury rooms, a spa, an infinity pool, and gourmet restaurants.
  - Prices start at €300 per night.

4. **Hotel Vistabella:** Located in Roses, overlooking the Bay of Roses - Offers magnificent accommodations with sea views, a spa, and Michelin-starred dining - Prices begin at €350 per night

5. Hostal de la Gavina GL: Located in S'Agaró, hidden within beautiful gardens overlooking the sea - Offers luxury rooms, a spa, outdoor pools, and gourmet dining - Prices start at €400 per night.

CHAPTER 4: TOP ATTRACTIONS IN COSTA BRAVA

1. **Dalí Theatre-Museum (Figueres):** Discover Salvador Dalí's surreal universe via the museum's extensive collection of paintings, sculptures, and installations.

2. **Cap de Creus Natural Park:** Explore the rough beauty of Costa Brava's coastline at this

breathtaking natural park, which is famed for its steep cliffs, secluded bays, and distinctive rock formations. Don't pass up the chance to explore the easternmost point of continental Spain.

3. Tossa de Mar: Discover the charming village of Tossa de Mar, which has a medieval old town protected by historic walls. Visit the magnificent Vila Vella fortification, walk along the picturesque waterfront promenade, and relax on the stunning beaches.

4. Cadaqués: Discover the bohemian appeal of Cadaqués, a charming seaside community that inspired artists such as Salvador Dalí and Pablo Picasso. Wander through its small alleyways, explore the medieval church of Santa Maria,

and take in the stunning views of the Mediterranean Sea.

5. Girona Old Town: Take a step back in time as you walk through Girona's ancient alleyways. Explore Girona's Cathedral, the Jewish Quarter, and the colorful buildings along the Onyar River.

6. **Empúries Archaeological Site:** Discover Costa Brava's history by exploring the remains of an ancient Greek and Roman city. The highlights include well-preserved mosaics, temples, and an amphitheater.

7. **Besalú:** Explore the old town of Besalú, renowned for its intact Romanesque architecture and lovely scenery. Discover attractions including the medieval bridge, Jewish baths, and the 11th-century Church of Sant Pere.

8. **Coves de Serinya:** Go on an underground journey to the Coves de Serinya, a network of caverns with stunning stalactites and stalagmites. Guided tours provide information about the geological structures and history of the caverns.

9. **Sant Pere de Rodes Monastery:** Explore the historic Sant Pere de Rodes Monastery, which sits on a hill overlooking the Costa Brava seashore. Explore the monastery's Romanesque architecture, cloisters, and panoramic views of the surrounding area.

10. **Botanical Gardens of Cap Roig:** Immerse yourself in the beauty of nature in the Botanical Gardens of Cap Roig, which is known for its rich array of Mediterranean flora and breathtaking sea vistas.

Beaches and Coastal Towns

Top Beaches

1. Calella de Palafrugell: This picturesque fishing village boasts several small sandy coves surrounded by rocky cliffs and turquoise waters, including the popular El Golfet and Port Bo beaches.

2. Tossa de Mar: Tossa de Mar is home to a stunning crescent-shaped beach with golden sand and crystal-clear waters, overlooked by the historic Vila Vella fortress.

3. Llafranc: Llafranc's pristine beach is backed by a charming promenade lined with restaurants and cafes, offering panoramic views of the Mediterranean Sea and the surrounding cliffs.

4. Cala Sa Conca (S'Agaró): This secluded cove is known for its tranquil atmosphere, clear waters, and scenic surroundings, making it a perfect spot for relaxation and snorkeling.

5. Platja d'Aro: Platja d'Aro boasts a long stretch of sandy beach with shallow waters, ideal for families and water sports enthusiasts. The

bustling promenade is lined with shops, bars, and restaurants.

Top Coastal Towns

1. **Cadaqués:** Known for its whitewashed buildings, narrow streets, and artistic heritage, Cadaqués exudes a bohemian charm. Explore

the town's waterfront promenade, art galleries, and the historic Church of Santa Maria.

2. Roses: Located on the northern end of Costa Brava, Roses offers a mix of sandy beaches, historic sites, and modern amenities. Visit the ancient ruins of Empúries and enjoy panoramic views from the Santa Rosa Castle.

3. Begur: Perched on a hilltop overlooking the Mediterranean Sea, Begur is known for its medieval castle, colorful houses, and stunning panoramic views. Explore the town's winding streets, visit its picturesque coves, and discover hidden gems like Sa Tuna and Aiguablava.

4. Blanes: Blanes is a vibrant coastal town known for its lively atmosphere, beautiful beaches, and the stunning Marimurtra

Botanical Garden. Don't miss the annual Blanes International Fireworks Competition, held in July.

5. L'Escala: L'Escala is a charming fishing village with a rich maritime history. Explore its sandy beaches, ancient ruins of Empúries, and sample fresh seafood at local restaurants along the waterfront promenade.

Natural Parks

1. **Cap de Creus Natural Park:** Cap de Creus Natural Park is located on Catalonia's northeastern point and is known for its jagged coastline, steep cliffs, and secret bays. Visitors may explore gorgeous hiking routes, discover unusual rock formations, and take in stunning views of the Mediterranean Sea. Don't miss the famous Cap de Creus Lighthouse and the charming hamlet of Cadaqués.

2. **Aiguamolls de l'Empordà Natural Park:** This wetland region, located near Roses, is well-known for its biodiversity and birding possibilities. Visitors may explore the park's path system, see a variety of bird species, and learn about the significance of wetland protection. The park also has rice fields,

marshes, and dunes, which provide home for a variety of plant and animal species.

3. **Montgrí, Medes Islands, and Baix Ter Natural Park:** The coastal natural park includes the Montgrí Massif, the Medes Islands archipelago, and the Baix Ter wetlands. It has a wide variety of scenery, including rough mountains, pristine beaches, and marine habitats. Visitors may trek to the top of Montgrí Castle for panoramic views, discover the aquatic environment surrounding the Medes Islands, and see birds in the Baix Ter wetlands.

4. **Aiguaviva Park:** Aiguaviva Park, near the town of Lloret de Mar, is a protected area with rich flora, natural springs, and picturesque pathways. Visitors may stroll through oak and pine woods, see secret waterfalls and streams,

and have picnics in tranquil settings. The park also provides possibilities for birding and animal viewing.

5. **Montseny Natural Park:** Despite being somewhat inland from Costa Brava, Montseny Natural Park is easily accessible and provides a verdant respite from the shore. This UNESCO Biosphere Reserve has lush woods, rocky mountains, and attractive valleys. Visitors may hike paths, see picturesque mountain communities, and appreciate the park's unique flora and animals.

CHAPTER 5: EXPLORING COSTA BRAVA'S REGIONS

1. Baix Empordà: Located in the south of Costa Brava, Baix Empordà is renowned for its charming coastal villages, lovely beaches, and rolling terrain. Discover lovely communities like Pals, Peratallada, and Begur, see ancient places like Empúries ruins, and take leisurely walks along the shore.

2. **Alt Empordà:** Located in the northern portion of Costa Brava, Alt Empordà has a rough coastline, beautiful beaches, and picturesque surroundings. Explore the lovely village of Cadaqués, the Cap de Creus Natural Park, and historical sites like the Sant Pere de Rodes Monastery.

3. **La Selva:** La Selva is an interior district of Costa Brava known for its lush woods, rolling hills, and attractive ancient towns. Explore Santa Coloma de Farners, the breathtaking Santa Clotilde Gardens in Lloret de Mar, and the Montseny Natural Park.

4. **Gironès:** Gironès is an area renowned for its ancient cities, cultural treasures, and picturesque landscape. Discover the historic alleyways of Girona's Old Town, sites like

Girona Cathedral and Arab Baths, and lovely villages like Monells and Besalú.

5. Ripollès: Located inland from Costa Brava, Ripollès is a hilly area renowned for its beautiful beauty, outdoor activities, and historic monuments. Discover the charming village of Camprodon, the breathtaking Vall de Núria valley, and the mountainous Pyrenees.

6. Pla de l'Estany: Pla de l'Estany is a tranquil area famed for its lush plains, quaint towns, and natural beauty. Discover the ancient town of Banyoles, the scenic Lake Banyoles, and hidden jewels such as the hamlet of Besalú and the volcanic territory of La Garrotxa.

Costa Brava's Coastal Gems

1. Calella de Palafrugell: This picturesque fishing community is noted for its whitewashed cottages, rugged shoreline, and stunning beaches. Explore secret coves like Cala del Golfet and Cala Port Bo by using a picturesque coastal route (Camí de Ronda).

2. Tossa de Mar: Tossa de Mar is home to one of the most magnificent beaches on the Costa Brava, with a vast crescent of golden sand surrounded by ancient walls and a gorgeous old town. Discover the ancient Vila Vella (Old Town) and unwind on the sandy beaches of Platja Gran.

3. Cadaqués: This bohemian beach community is known for its whitewashed houses, tiny lanes, and breathtaking ocean vistas. Discover the picturesque town center, visit the Dalí House Museum, and relax on the surrounding beaches of Portlligat and Playa Es Poal.

4. Begur: Begur is bordered by some of the most stunning beaches and coves on the Costa Brava. Discover isolated jewels like Aiguablava, Sa

Riera, and Platja Fonda, each with pure waters and breathtaking natural scenery.

5. Llafranc: This attractive coastal town has a wonderful sandy beach, a stunning promenade, and quaint waterfront eateries. Enjoy panoramic views from the Sant Sebastià Lighthouse and visit neighboring sites such as the Botanical Gardens of Cap Roig.

6. Blanes: Blanes is renowned for its extensive sandy beaches, lively waterfront promenade, and breathtaking Marimurtra Botanical Garden. Enjoy the beaches of Platja de Blanes and Platja de S'Abanell, or explore the rocky coves along the Camí de Ronda.

7. Roses: Roses has a variety of sandy beaches, rocky coves, and historical sites. Visit the

beautiful beaches of Platja de Roses and Platja de la Punta, or go into the adjacent Cap de Creus Natural Park to discover rough coastal scenery and hidden jewels.

8. L'Escala: This little fishing community has a picturesque coastline filled with sandy beaches and rocky coves. Visit the historic old town, ancient remains of Empúries, and relax on beaches like Cala Montgó and Platja de Riells.

CHAPTER 6: CULINARY DELIGHTS

1. Seafood: As a coastal region, Costa Brava is renowned for its fresh and flavorful seafood dishes. Indulge in locally caught fish such as anchovies, sardines, and sea bream, prepared in a variety of ways including grilled, fried, or marinated in vinegar.

2. Suquet de Peix: This traditional Catalan fish stew is a must-try dish in Costa Brava. Made with a variety of fresh fish, potatoes, tomatoes, garlic, and saffron, Suquet de Peix is hearty, aromatic, and bursting with flavor.

3. Fideuà: Similar to paella but made with short noodles instead of rice, Fideuà is a popular dish in Costa Brava. It typically features a variety of seafood such as shrimp, squid, and mussels, cooked with noodles in a rich and savory broth.

4. Botifarra amb Mongetes: This traditional Catalan dish consists of grilled sausage served with white beans. It's a simple yet delicious dish that showcases the flavors of the region's locally sourced ingredients.

5. **Pa amb Tomàquet:** A staple of Catalan cuisine, Pa amb Tomàquet is a simple yet flavorful dish made with crusty bread, ripe tomatoes, garlic, and olive oil. It's often served as a side dish or appetizer and pairs well with a variety of other Catalan specialties.

6. **Crema Catalana:** This creamy and delicious dessert is a Catalan version of crème brûlée. Made with milk, sugar, egg yolks, and flavored with cinnamon and lemon zest, Crema Catalana is typically served cold with a caramelized sugar crust on top.

7. **Empordà Wines:** Costa Brava is home to the Empordà wine region, known for producing high-quality wines with unique flavors and characteristics. Sample a variety of reds, whites,

and rosés made from local grape varieties such as Garnacha, Carignan, and Macabeo.

8. Catalan Pastries: Treat yourself to a selection of traditional Catalan pastries and sweets, including xuixos (deep-fried pastries filled with cream), panellets (almond-based cookies), and mel i mató (fresh cheese drizzled with honey).

Wine & Dine in Style

1. Fine eating Restaurants: Begin your gastronomic adventure by eating at one of Costa Brava's famous fine dining establishments. These restaurants provide magnificent dishes made by outstanding chefs, with inventive interpretations of Catalan cuisine employing the best local products. For an exceptional dining

experience, try Michelin-starred restaurants like El Celler de Can Roca in Girona or Les Cols in Olot.

2. Winery Tours and Tastings: Discover Costa Brava's wine area by visiting local wineries and vineyards. Take guided tours to learn about the winemaking process, from grape cultivation to barrel aging, and enjoy a selection of great wines. The Empordà Wine Route has many wineries to explore, including Mas Oller, Perelada, and Terra Remota.

3. Gourmet culinary Markets: Discover the unique culinary culture of Costa Brava by visiting local markets. Visit lively markets like Mercat de la Boqueria in Barcelona or Mercat de Sant Josep in Girona to find a diverse selection of fresh fruit, artisanal cheeses, cured

meats, and other gastronomic pleasures. Pick up picnic fixings or sample local delights.

4. **Culinary Workshops & Cooking lessons:** Learn more about Catalan cuisine via hands-on cooking lessons and workshops. Learn how to make classic foods like paella, seafood tapas, and Catalan sweets under the supervision of skilled chefs. These interactive experiences provide insight into local culinary methods, ingredients, and tastes.

5. **Beachfront Dining:** For a fantastic dining experience against a breathtaking setting, visit one of Costa Brava's beachfront restaurants. Enjoy delicious seafood and Mediterranean cuisine while admiring the beautiful waves of the Mediterranean Sea. Llafranc, Calella de

Palafrugell, and Tossa de Mar are three popular coastal eating spots.

6. Gastronomic Festivals and Events: Time your visit to coincide with one of Costa Brava's culinary festivals and events. These events, which range from seafood festivals to wine tastings and culinary contests, honor the region's culinary legacy while also highlighting the abilities of local chefs and producers. Check the calendar for festivities like the Girona Gastronomy Festival and the Cap Roig Festival.

Recommended Restaurants

1. **El Celler de Can Roca (Girona):** Recognized as one of the world's top restaurants, El Celler de Can Roca provides an outstanding eating experience. The restaurant, run by the Roca brothers, delivers unique and imaginative Catalan cuisine with a contemporary touch. Reservations are necessary.

2. **Les Cols (Olot):** Located in the heart of the volcanic area of La Garrotxa, Les Cols is a Michelin-starred restaurant recognized for its simple design and outstanding tasting menus. Chef Fina Puigdevall's inventive recipes showcase local ingredients and tastes.

3. **Miramar (Llançà):** Located on the magnificent Costa Brava coastline, Miramar is a

Michelin-starred restaurant famed for its innovative food and spectacular views of the Mediterranean Sea. Chef Paco Pérez mixes traditional Catalan recipes with cutting-edge methods to produce outstanding meals.

4. Casamar (Llafranc): Located in the lovely seaside village of Llafranc, Casamar is a Michelin-starred restaurant that serves modern Catalan cuisine with an emphasis on seafood and local ingredients. Enjoy breathtaking views of the sea while sampling Chef Quim Casellas' inventive meals.

5. Massana (Girona): Massana, a family-run restaurant in the ancient city of Girona, serves traditional Catalan food with a contemporary touch. Chef Pere Massana's seasonal tasting

menus reflect regional tastes, with a focus on fresh, locally sourced ingredients.

6. **Els Tinars (Llagostera):** Located in a beautifully renovated farmhouse surrounded by lush grounds, Els Tinars is a Michelin-starred restaurant renowned for its exquisite environment and excellent food. Chef Pere Arpa creates a cuisine based on traditional Catalan dishes with a modern twist.

7. **Ca l'Enric (La Vall de Bianya):** Nestled in the scenic countryside of La Garrotxa, Ca l'Enric is a family-owned restaurant recognized for its welcoming atmosphere and delectable food. Chef Joan Vehí uses locally available ingredients to create meals that highlight regional tastes.

8. Sa Punta (Pals): Sa Punta, perched on a cliff overlooking the Mediterranean Sea, serves exquisite Mediterranean food and provides panoramic views. Enjoy fresh seafood, grilled meats, and traditional Catalan cuisine while admiring the breathtaking coastline environment.

Festivals & Celebrations

1. Spring (April-June)

-Festival of Sant Jordi (April 23rd): This national holiday celebrates Catalonia's patron saint, St. George. Expect book fairs, rose gifting traditions, and lively street performances throughout Costa Brava.

-L'Escala's Asparagus Fair (April-May): This gastronomic delight celebrates the prized white asparagus of El Empordà region. Sample delicious asparagus dishes, witness cooking demonstrations, and learn about local agricultural traditions.

-Girona Flower Festival (May): The historic city of Girona transforms into a floral wonderland during this annual festival. Streets are adorned with colorful displays, balconies overflow with blooms, and flower markets come alive with vibrant hues.

2. Summer (July-August)

-Porta Ferrada Festival (Sant Feliu de Guixols, July-August): This prestigious music festival attracts international artists across various genres, from classical and jazz to pop and rock.

Enjoy open-air concerts in the historic setting of the town's medieval monastery.

-Cap Roig Festival (Calella de Palafrugell, July-August): Another renowned music festival held in the stunning Cap Roig botanical gardens. The picturesque setting and diverse music lineup make this a truly unforgettable experience.

-Festival Castell de Peralada (Peralada, July-August): Immerse yourself in a world of opera, classical music, dance, and theater performances held within the majestic Peralada Castle.

-Palamos Shrimp Festival (Palamos, July): A delicious celebration of the local Palamós shrimp, a regional delicacy. Enjoy freshly caught shrimp cooked in various ways, cooking demonstrations, and lively street entertainment.

3. Autumn (September-October)

-Temps de Flors (Girona, September): Girona's courtyards and historical monuments are transformed into breathtaking floral installations during this unique festival. Wander through the city's charming streets and marvel at the creativity and artistry on display.

-Festival Cruïlla (Barcelona, Late September): While not technically in Costa Brava, this major music festival held near Barcelona is easily accessible and attracts a stellar lineup of international artists across various genres.

-Begur International Film Festival (Begur, October): Cinema enthusiasts flock to Begur for this independent film festival showcasing works from around the globe. Enjoy screenings in historical settings and participate in workshops and discussions.

4. Winter (November-March)

-Living Nativity Scenes (Various Towns, December): Experience the Christmas spirit with traditional nativity scenes recreated in various towns throughout Costa Brava. Often life-sized and featuring local residents, these scenes offer a glimpse into regional Christmas traditions.

-Three Kings Parade (January 5th): The arrival of the Three Kings is a major celebration in Spain. Witness lively parades with elaborate floats, music, and children eagerly awaiting their gifts.

Tips for Festival Goers

- Purchase tickets for major festivals well in advance, especially during peak season.

- Research local customs and dress codes for specific festivals if applicable.

- Embrace the festive spirit! Costa Brava's celebrations are a vibrant way to connect with the local culture and create lasting memories.

CHAPTER 7: ACTIVITIES AND ADVENTURES

1. Beach Hopping: With over 200 kilometers of coastline, Costa Brava has countless beautiful beaches and quiet coves waiting to be discovered. Spend your days basking in the sun, swimming in crystal-clear seas, and resting on

the sandy beaches of Platja de Pals, Cala Montgó, and Cala Sa Tuna.

2. **Water Sports:** Dive into the seas of Costa Brava to participate in a range of water sports and activities. Explore the region's diverse marine life and underwater vistas by snorkeling or scuba diving. Kayaking, paddleboarding, and windsurfing are additional popular ways to explore the shoreline.

3. **Coastal Hiking:** Put on your hiking boots and explore gorgeous coastal routes with stunning views of the Mediterranean Sea. The Camí de Ronda is a coastal walk that runs along the Costa Brava coastline. It offers chances for peaceful strolls or demanding excursions over steep terrain and secret bays.

4. **Cultural Sightseeing:** Discover Costa Brava's rich cultural legacy by visiting ancient cities, picturesque villages, and architectural sites. Explore Girona's Old Town, Empúries' ruins, and the region's Romanesque churches and castles.

5. **Winery Tours and Tastings:** Learn about Costa Brava's world-renowned wines by visiting local wineries and vineyards. Take guided tours to learn about the winemaking process, from grape cultivation to bottling, and drink a selection of exquisite wines, including the region's renowned Empordà wines.

6. **Cycling Adventures:** On a riding excursion in Costa Brava, you'll pass through stunning landscapes, attractive towns, and seaside trails. The area has a network of cycling routes

appropriate for all skill levels, from relaxing rides through vineyards to tough mountain trails in the Pyrenees foothills.

7. Adventure Parks: For adrenaline-pumping entertainment, go to one of Costa Brava's adventure parks, where you can zipline through the trees, tackle obstacle courses, and test your agility with aerial challenges. Adventure parks such as Costa Brava Parc Aventura and Parc Aventura provide thrills for the whole family.

8. Cultural Festivals and Events: Get involved in Costa Brava's dynamic cultural scene by visiting local festivals and events. From music festivals and culinary fairs to traditional festivities and art exhibits, Costa Brava has plenty to keep you entertained and inspired at all times.

Water Sports and Beach Activities

1. Snorkeling: Explore Costa Brava's diverse marine life and underwater scenery by snorkeling in the crystal-clear seas. For good snorkeling chances, visit coves and rocky regions like Cala Montgó, Cala Sa Tuna, and Cap de Creus Natural Park.

2. Scuba Diving: Take a scuba diving adventure along the Costa Brava shoreline to discover hidden gems under the surface. Dive locations including Medes Islands Marine Reserve, Aiguablava, and Illes Formigues have different marine habitats, vivid reefs, and underwater caverns to discover.

3. Kayaking: Paddle around Costa Brava's scenic coastline to discover secret coves, sea caves, and isolated beaches via kayak. Guided kayak trips are provided for all ability levels, enabling you to see the region's natural beauty from a new viewpoint.

4. Stand-up Paddleboarding (SUP): Glide over the tranquil seas of Costa Brava on a stand-up paddleboard, taking in panoramic views of the coastline. SUP is a popular pastime for people

of all ages and ability levels, since it provides a pleasant opportunity to explore the beach while also exercising.

5. Windsurfing: Experience the excitement of windsurfing on Costa Brava's windy beaches, where optimal conditions greet fans of this exciting sea activity. Visit Roses, Sant Pere Pescador, or Platja de Pals for great windsurfing conditions and equipment rentals.

6. Jet Skiing: Get your heart racing with a jet skiing trip along the Costa Brava shoreline. Rent a jet ski and speed over the waves, having the freedom to explore the shore at your leisure.

7. Parasailing: Fly far above the shore and take in the beautiful aerial views of Costa Brava when parasailing. Experience the exhilaration

of flight as you glide through the air, taking in panoramic views of the Mediterranean Sea and stunning coastal surroundings.

8. **Beach Volleyball:** Relax on the sandy beaches of Costa Brava and play a fun game of beach volleyball with friends and family. Many beaches have dedicated volleyball courts where you may challenge each other to a game or participate in a pickup match with other beachgoers.

Hiking and Cycling Routes

Hiking routes

1. Camí de Ronda: This ancient coastal walk spans the whole Costa Brava coastline, providing breathtaking views of the Mediterranean Sea and access to secret coves and beaches. The path is separated into portions, enabling hikers to select between

shorter and longer excursions depending on their inclinations.

2. **Cap de Creus Natural Park:** A network of hiking routes leads you across the park's rocky headlands and stunning scenery. Highlights include a trek to the Cap de Creus lighthouse, as well as pathways leading to isolated beaches and seaside vistas.

3. **Garrotxa Volcanic Zone Natural Park:** Hike along a range of pathways to explore the park's distinctive volcanic landscape. Walk through lush woods, past old volcanic cones, and down river valleys to discover the park's rich flora and animals.

4. **Montseny Natural Park:** Montseny Natural Park, located inland from Costa Brava, has a

variety of hiking paths that go through lush woods, picturesque meadows, and rocky summits. Montseny Mountain's peak offers magnificent views of the surrounding area.

5. Sant Aniol d'Aguja: This lovely region near Sadernes has a beautiful canyon and waterfall, making it a favorite trekking destination. Follow the river walk to the waterfall, where you may cool yourself in the natural pools.

Cycle Routes

1. Greenways (Vies Verdes): Costa Brava's network of greenways follows old railway lines and provides picturesque cycling routes through rural, woods, and seaside environments. The Girona-Olot Greenway and the Carrilet II Greenway are popular routes with cyclists of all skill levels.

2. **Empordà Cycle Route:** Discover the stunning Empordà area by cycling through lovely towns, vineyards, and olive groves. As you bike through the Catalan countryside, enjoy the level terrain and well-marked routes.

3. **Gavarres Massif:** The Gavarres Massif provides hard mountain riding tracks across rocky terrain and deep woods. Follow paths that wind across the mountain, conquering difficult climbs and exhilarating descents while admiring panoramic views of the surrounding area.

4. **Ruta del Carrilet:** A flat and picturesque cycling route between Girona and Sant Feliu de Guíxols, following the line of a former narrow-gauge railway. The path travels through

picturesque towns and provides possibilities to see historical attractions along the way.

5. Costa Brava Coastal Path: Take a leisurely bike ride along the Costa Brava Coastal Path, which follows the Camí de Ronda hiking track. Enjoy breathtaking sea views and access to secluded coves and beaches along the route.

CHAPTER 8: NIGHTLIFE

1. **Lively coastal Bars:** Many of Costa Brava's coastal villages come alive at night, with beach bars and clubs serving drinks, live music, and DJ performances. Enjoy a refreshing drink while soaking up the sea air and dancing the night away on the sandy sands of prominent beach spots such as Lloret de Mar, Platja d'Aro, and Tossa de Mar.

2. **Waterfront Promenades:** Take a stroll along the waterfront promenades of Costa Brava's coastal towns and cities, where you'll discover a variety of pubs, restaurants, and cafés with outdoor seating and breathtaking views of the Mediterranean. Enjoy a relaxing drink or tapas while seeing the sunset over the sea.

3. **Nightclubs and Discos:** Costa Brava has a thriving nightlife culture, with various nightclubs and discos located across the area. Clubs such as Pacha La Pineda in Lloret de Mar, Disco Tropics in Platja d'Aro, and Sala Beach Club in Roses host dance parties till dawn with the newest rhythms and electronic music.

4. **Music Venues and Concerts:** Costa Brava's music venues and cultural centers provide live music performances and concerts. Costa Brava's music culture is constantly evolving, with everything from tiny jazz clubs and rock pubs to bigger concert venues and outdoor amphitheaters.

5. **Festivals and Events:** Costa Brava offers a number of festivals and events throughout the year, allowing visitors to enjoy the region's

dynamic cultural scene after dark. Costa Brava offers a variety of entertainment options, including music festivals, street parties, cultural festivities, and fireworks displays.

6. **Casinos and Gaming:** If you're feeling fortunate, Costa Brava has a number of casinos and gaming venues where you may play poker, blackjack, roulette, and slots. Test your talents and have a thrilling night in casinos such as Gran Casino Costa Brava in Lloret de Mar and Casino Castell de Peralada in Peralada.

7. **Tapas Bars and Restaurants:** Discover the local culinary scene by trying classic Spanish tapas and regional delicacies at Costa Brava's tapas bars and restaurants. Many restaurants remain open late, enabling you to savor

wonderful cuisine and beverages into the early hours.

Shopping

1. **Local Markets:** Discover the vibrant local markets that take place in cities and villages around Costa Brava. From weekly farmers' markets selling fresh fruit and artisanal items to flea markets selling antiques and vintage discoveries, there is something for everyone to enjoy. Don't miss the Mercat de la Boqueria in Barcelona or the Mercat de la Llibertat in Girona for a lively shopping adventure.

2. **Artisanal Crafts:** Costa Brava is famed for its rich artisanal tradition, and you'll discover a range of locally crafted crafts and souvenirs to

take home as keepsakes from your stay. Look for handcrafted ceramics, textiles, jewelry, and pottery manufactured by local craftsmen in workshops and stores around the area.

3. Designer Fashion: If you're looking for some retail therapy, visit Costa Brava's posh shopping areas and designer stores. Cities like Barcelona and Girona are home to well-known fashion companies, luxury shops, and department stores where you can find the newest trends and designer labels.

4. Coastal Towns and Resorts: Visit Costa Brava's lovely coastal towns and resorts, which provide a variety of seaside stores and boutiques offering beachwear, swimwear, and souvenirs. Stroll around the seaside promenades of Cadaqués, Tossa de Mar, and

Llafranc, stopping at stores for one-of-a-kind treasures and presents.

5. **Culinary Delights:** Bring home a taste of Costa Brava by shopping for local delicacies and gourmet items. Visit specialist food stores and markets to load up on olive oil, wine, cheese, cured meats, and other Catalan delicacies to enjoy at home or give as presents to friends and family.

6. **Shopping Centers:** For a convenient and contemporary shopping experience, go to one of Costa Brava's shopping centers or malls. Places like La Roca Village in Barcelona and Espai Gironès in Girona provide a variety of stores, restaurants, and entertainment choices under one roof.

7. **Arts and Antiques:** Explore the old towns and villages of Costa Brava to find art galleries, antique shops, and vintage stores. Discover one-of-a-kind artworks, collectibles, and gems reflecting the region's cultural history and creative flare.

CHAPTER 9: PRACTICAL INFORMATION

1. **Visa Requirements:** Before visiting Costa Brava, make sure you understand the visa requirements for your nationality. EU nationals may enter Spain, including Costa Brava, with a valid passport or identification card. Non-EU nationals may need a visa, so make sure you

have the relevant papers well in advance of your trip.

2. Currency: The Euro (€) is the currency used in Costa Brava and across Spain. ATMs are extensively distributed across towns and cities, and credit cards are commonly accepted. However, it is always a good idea to have some cash on hand for minor purchases and in case of need.

3. Language: Although Spanish is the official language of Spain, Catalan is widely spoken across the area, particularly in places such as Girona. Although English is widely spoken in tourist regions, learning a few basic Spanish phrases can help you converse with the people.

4. Weather: Costa Brava has a Mediterranean climate, which means scorching summers and pleasant winters. Summer (June to August) is the busiest tourist season, with average temperatures ranging from 25 to 30°C (77-86°F). Spring (April-May) and fall (September-October) provide good weather and less people, making them great seasons to visit.

5. Transportation: Costa Brava's well-developed transportation network makes it quite simple to get about. Although renting a vehicle is a popular way to explore the area on your own, buses, trains, and taxis are all accessible. The Girona-Costa Brava Airport is the primary gateway for foreign passengers.

6. Health and Safety: Costa Brava is typically a safe place for tourists, but you must take

common-sense steps to protect your safety. Make sure you have travel insurance that includes medical expenditures and emergency evacuation. The European Health Insurance Card (EHIC) may allow EU nationals to receive state-provided healthcare.

7. Electricity: The standard voltage throughout Spain, including Costa Brava, is 230V at a frequency of 50Hz. Electrical outlets utilize the European standard Type C two-pin plug, therefore you may require an adaptor if you're coming from a nation with a different plug type.

8. Local traditions: Learn about local traditions and manners to guarantee a polite and pleasurable visit in Costa Brava. Spain has a laid-back culture, however it is customary to

greet someone with a handshake or a kiss on the cheek (air kiss) when meeting for the first time.

CHAPTER 10: BEYOND COSTA BRAVA

1. Barcelona: As Catalonia's dynamic capital, Barcelona has a plethora of attractions, including renowned monuments such as the Sagrada Familia, Park Güell, and Las Ramblas. Explore the city's ancient districts, try Catalan food at local markets, and enjoy the vibrant atmosphere of this international metropolis.

2. Girona: Located only a short drive from Costa Brava, Girona is a lovely city famed for its well-preserved medieval district, colorful buildings along the Onyar River, and majestic Gothic cathedral. Wander through small cobblestone lanes, see the Jewish Quarter, and climb the city walls for panoramic vistas.

3. Cadaqués: This charming seaside town, on the Cap de Creus peninsula, is known for its whitewashed buildings, tiny alleyways, and stunning coastline. Explore the lovely old town, see the Salvador Dalí House-Museum, and relax on the gorgeous beaches nearby.

4. Figueres: Art fans can visit Figueres, the birthplace of surrealist artist Salvador Dalí. The Dalí Theatre-Museum is a surreal masterpiece constructed by the artist and houses a comprehensive collection of his works from his entire career.

5. Montserrat: Head inland to see the breathtaking Montserrat mountain range, which is home to the famed Benedictine abbey of Santa Maria de Montserrat. Take a picturesque cable car journey to the highland

refuge, where you can enjoy panoramic views of the surrounding countryside and wander along gorgeous pathways.

6. **Costa Dorada:** Located south of Costa Brava, the Costa Dorada is famed for its golden sandy beaches, attractive coastal villages, and family-friendly resorts. Visit the Roman city of Tarragona, visit the picturesque fishing hamlet of Cambrils, or relax on Salou's beaches.

7. **Pyrenees Mountains:** Nature lovers and outdoor enthusiasts may go inland to see the rugged beauty of the Pyrenees Mountains. Hike through magnificent national parks, ski in the winter, or explore charming mountain communities like La Seu d'Urgell and Puigcerdà.

8. **Wine Country:** Catalonia is home to numerous well-known wine districts, including the Penedès, Priorat, and Empordà. Take a wine tour to see vineyards, taste local varietals, and learn about Catalan winemaking traditions.

Insider Tips And Local Insights

1. **Discover Off-the-Beaten Path Villages:** While well-known places like Lloret de Mar and Tossa

de Mar are unquestionably gorgeous, try stepping off the main road to visit lesser-known communities like Calella de Palafrugell, Begur, and Pals. These lovely seaside communities include scenic streets, secret coves, and a more relaxed vibe.

2. **Visit During Shoulder Seasons:** While summer is the most popular tourist season in Costa Brava, consider going during the shoulder seasons of spring (April to May) and autumn (September to October). You'll enjoy cooler weather, less tourists, and reduced lodging costs while enjoying admiring the region's beauty.

3. **Try Local Cuisine in Traditional Taverns:** Skip the tourist traps and go to traditional pubs and small restaurants called "bodegas" or "masias" for true Catalan food. Dessert options

include "mar i muntanya" (sea and mountain), "fideuà" (similar to paella but served with noodles), and "crema catalana" (Catalan cream).

4. **Discover Hidden Beaches and Calas:** Costa Brava is home to many hidden coves and isolated beaches that are often ignored by visitors. Rent a kayak or stroll along the Camí de Ronda coastal trail to uncover hidden beauties like Cala Estreta, Cala Castell, or Cala del Crit.

5. **Experience Local Festivals and customs:** Participate in local festivals and customs to learn about Costa Brava's rich cultural history. From colorful fiestas and traditional dances to medieval fairs and wine festivals, there's always something going on in the area.

6. **Embrace Slow Travel:** Costa Brava is best enjoyed at a leisurely pace, so take your time and enjoy the relaxed environment. Spend your relaxing days drinking coffee at sidewalk cafés, browsing local markets, or just admiring the breathtaking coastline landscape.

7. **Interact with Locals:** Start talks with locals to learn about the region's culture, history, and way of life. Engaging with locals, whether it's conversing with fishermen at the market or sharing pleasantries with store owners, may lead to memorable and unique interactions.

8. **Respect the Environment:** Costa Brava's natural beauty is its most valuable asset, therefore please respect the environment throughout your stay. To have the least influence on delicate ecosystems, dispose of

garbage ethically, avoid single-use plastics, and stick to designated routes.

Useful Phrases

Greetings and Common Courtesy

- Bon dia (bon dee-ah): Good morning
- Bon vespre (bon ves-pra): Good evening
- Hola (oh-la): Hello
- Adéu (a-deu): Goodbye
- Si us plau (si us plau): Please
- Gràcies (grah-see-es): Thank you
- De res (de res): You're welcome
- Perdó (per-do): Excuse me

Basic Needs

- M'ho pot repetir, si us plau? (m'ho pot repe-tir, si us plau): Can you repeat that, please?
- No entenc (no en-tenc): I don't understand
- Parla anglès? (par-la ang-les): Do you speak English?
- Quant val això? (quant val ay-sho): How much is this?
- Tinc una reserva (tin-ca una re-ser-va): I have a reservation

Directions

- On és el lavabo? (on es el la-va-bo): Where is the toilet?
- On puc trobar...? (on puc tro-bar...?): Where can I find...?
- A l'esquerra (a les-kera): Left
- A la dreta (a la dre-ta): Right

- Recte (rec-ta): Straight

Food and Drinks

- Una cervesa, si us plau (u-na ser-ve-sa, si us plau): A beer, please
- Un cafè, si us plau (un ca-fè, si us plau): A coffee, please
- L' compte, si us plau (el comp-te, si us plau): The check, please
- Bon profit! (bon pro-fit!): Enjoy your meal!

Numbers (1-10)

- U (u): One
- Dos (dos): Two
- Tres (tres): Three
- Quatre (kwa-tre): Four
- Cinc (sinc): Five
- Sis (sis): Six

- Set (set): Seven
- Vuit (vuit): Eight
- Nou (nou): Nine
- Deu (deu): Ten

Printed in Great Britain
by Amazon